THINGS THAT MAKE A BUSINESS SUCCESSFUL:

SALES, MARKETING, AND CUSTOMER SERVES, DELIVERING AN AMAZING USER EXPERIENCE AT EACH AND EVERY INTERACTION POINT

By

MARCEL R. LUTE

Copyright

Author Page

The perceptive author of "Things that Make Business Successful," Marcel R. Lute, provides a plethora of knowledge and experience to the field of business success. In this fascinating investigation, Lute explores the subtleties that distinguish successful companies. Using his extensive experience in business, he reveals the fundamental ideas that propel success, placing a strong emphasis on strategic vision, flexibility, and capable leadership. Lute's distinct viewpoint, developed over years of negotiating a variety of sectors, provides readers with useful advice on creating and maintaining successful businesses. Marcel R. Lute creates an engaging story that is a great resource for both seasoned and aspiring business owners. He has a sharp eye for market dynamics and a love for innovation. The Author page provides access to Lute's deep knowledge of business dynamics, which makes his writings a priceless tool for anybody trying to figure out how to achieve long-term success.

TABLE OF CONTENT

Introduction 4

Chapter 1:..16

Chapter 2:..26

Chapter 3:..33

Chapter 4:..43

Chapter 5:..58

Chapter 6:..65

Chapter 7:..74

Chapter 8:..96

Introduction

Why Building StoryBrand Marketing Framework is effective

Donald Miller, the CEO and creator of the marketing firm StoryBrand, created the distinctive marketing concept known as The StoryBrand Marketing. It's designed to help businesses use narrative techniques to clarify their marketing message.

Through a series of questions, The StoryBrand Marketing helps business owners who write content for their goods or services, produce films, or construct websites. Seven sections that follow a narrative format based on some of humankind's most cherished tales make up this set of questions.

Businesses invest a lot of effort and money into creating campaigns that are meant to attract new clients, but they often launch these projects without first taking the time to craft an engaging story. Without this basis, businesses may be passing up chances to connect with customers and other target groups more effectively. Creating a compelling tale aids firms in capturing interest, establishing trust, and increasing revenue.

I'm using Donald Miller as an example because he thinks businesses can improve the world by developing deep relationships with their customers.

By participating in one of the many seminars provided by StoryBrand, businesses may learn how to develop their story strategy. Both business owners and marketing professionals who wish to strengthen their company's narrative might benefit from these sessions. StoryBrand Marketing assists companies in condensing communications into the three crucial parts of every conversation:

- Who are i?
- Exactly How am I acting?
- Why is it important?

The StoryBrand Marketing was created in a way to assist businesses in telling their narrative in order to connect with customers more effectively. StoryBrand offers further consulting services that will aid clients in understanding the most effective ways to communicate their message, in addition to courses that direct business owners through the process of constructing a narrative. Businesses can enroll in one of StoryBrand's many classes or engage full-time consultants who have received training in the company's methods. Organizations are better equipped to engage target audiences and increase brand awareness when they receive assistance in developing a compelling story.

The StoryBrand was created to help businesses tell their brand's story in only a few words, which would help them win their customers' trust.

Why StoryBrand Is Successful

'Story marketing' is one of the marketing jargons you may have come across. Story marketing is the process of developing marketing materials that appeal to emotional themes, talk to your audience as individuals, and establish a more intimate connection with them.

Businesses have a useful tool for integrating brand tales into their marketing and advertising messages thanks to the StoryBrand marketing roadmap. Instead of cramming it with random information and figures, the framework develops cohesive marketing narratives about how your products and services enhance lives. Instead of relying on extravagant promises or inflated claims, marketing can deliver a powerful message by emphasizing how your brand improves living and what problems you solve.

The StoryBrand assists in developing marketing materials that are captivating enough to generate interest in your items without making exaggerated claims or overselling them. Marketing becomes considerably more persuasive while still being honest and trustworthy when you present tales that express clearly how your brand improves lives and then back up those claims to help a buyer see success.

One of the finest methods to develop a marketing message that prioritizes your clients is by using this strategy.

The StoryBrand assists companies in clearly communicating how their goods and services address issues in the customer's narrative. Because it enables businesses to communicate their message without getting buried in all the bells and whistles of technology, this marketing strategy has proven particularly successful in the field of tech marketing.

The brand's narrative is a key component of marketing. In order to succeed, it's critical that you successfully communicate with your customers about your values and how your product or service will help them prevent a disastrous outcome. By assisting businesses in developing messages that are compelling enough to pique a potential customer's interest in your brand without overselling your items, StoryBrand offers an efficient framework for doing just that. This strategy facilitates the creation of superior marketing materials from the ground up, which ultimately results ingenerate increased sales and successful outcomes for clients that benefit from your company's services!

A Fresh Call to Action

Utilizing the StoryBrand building, convey a message that is crystal clear.

The StoryBrand Framework is a straightforward seven-step procedure created to aid with message clarification. It's simple to develop a captivating brand story that will engage potential customers and help them understand why they require your product or service in their life once you have the framework down.

All of it begins with a BrandScript. The BrandScript is the blueprint that directs the words you'll employ, if the Framework is the road plan for your messaging.

When you use the StoryBrand to generate a compelling message, the BrandScript performs all the work.

The StoryBrand's Seven Components

There are seven sections in the StoryBrand. Each section focuses on a particular phase of creating or effectively communicating your story. The framework is made to make it easier for you to tell your narrative, engage with clients, and ultimately expand your business. There are seven sections so that each one can function independently as a separate reference for real-world use.

Following are the seven components of the StoryBrand building:

1.The Savior

The consumer is the protagonist in your tale! They want to believe that they are a special part of something, and that you are aware of their needs.

Your customer should ALWAYS be the focal point of your messaging. They are the primary driver of your brand's existence. It's not just polite to prioritize your customers, but it's also beneficial to your company's bottom line.

2. The Issue

In stories, heroes frequently experience difficulties, and your product might provide a solution. It's crucial to think about how they can solve their issues while offering answers or a greater interest in what you have to give so that we can all succeed together.

What issue do your clients wish to resolve? By empowering the customer and providing them with all the tools they need to address their problems through your brand, StoryBrand makes a required adjustment to the conventional method of marketing.

You won't be the one to rescue your consumer from their difficulties in this tale. When you make your consumer the hero, when they ultimately achieve, it will be more of an accomplishment for them and a success story worth telling.

3. The Manual

Just picture a world without a guide. We would be where? What might happen if you abandoned your clients to fend for themselves in the wilderness of chances and challenges in life, not even knowing which way success or safety lay? No, it doesn't have to be this way; brandishers are available to assist you and have been waiting nearby all along.

As the brand that both knows the way and is eager to reveal it to its clients, you play the role of the guide in this tale.

It is your responsibility as a guide to convey authority and empathy. Inform them that you are aware of their issue and that you are prepared to assist because you have done it in the past.

4. The Strategy

Customers can be confident that they won't be wandering through your business aimlessly with little knowledge of what's available if you have an excellent guide. A strategy considerably boosts their chances of making their purchase selection easy and provides a clear path to stability.

Any purchase carries some risk. The first thing your buyer wonders when they read your copy is, "Will this work?"

Giving them a strategy is one way to reduce the danger. Your role as the guide is to describe the procedure to them so that they can choose your brand. If they don't believe that working with you won't be difficult, they'll just dismiss your message.

5. The Request for Action

Only when they are confronted with a challenge will heroes act. This is accomplished in a number of ways, including motivating them with discounts or freebies, requesting their consent when necessary (depending on the circumstance), etc. This strategy's premise has consistently worked because people want what is right for them but need encouragement from others before taking action.

It's time for them to respond once you've given them as much value as you can. Make sure your CTAs are straightforward, clear, and simple to respond to.

6. The Failure Story

All businesses should prioritize preventing failure, but when you're in the business of publicizing your triumphs, it's extremely crucial. The stakes are higher than ever because everyone wants to avoid emotional tragedies or else risk losing clients who might never come back once word gets around town about what happened with whichever business caused them so much pain and suffering - even if those responsible were strictly external forces beyond our control!

7. The Story of Success

Although you are guiding the hero to victory, you still need to demonstrate how wonderful their future will be. Give your clients a vision that motivates them and delivers for working with you on business.

Use the StoryBrand Framework in Your Marketing Materials for These Advantages

Portraying Your Company's Actual Self

What you have in your hands is a business that is intended to be disregarded when you're marketing materials and brand message do not reflect your brand's genuine identity. Using the StoryBrand structure in marketing is a terrific method to assist in transforming marketing into a sales-driving success. The core idea behind the StoryBrand framework is to develop a brand narrative that will emotionally connect with customers and convince them to spend their time and money on your company's goods or services.

Your marketing materials should be clear.

You can make sure that your brand story is clearly communicated in all of your marketing materials, from print ads to social media postings, by establishing a unifying theme. This will inspire potential customers to contact you about making a purchase of your goods or services.

Gain the confidence of your audience.

You may build trust with your customers by changing your marketing materials from being product-focused to customer-focused. Maintaining brand consistency throughout all marketing materials can help you avoid losing the customer's trust and make sure they understand what they are signing up for when they subscribe to your service or buy one of your goods.

Having marketing materials that evoke an emotional response in potential clients will ultimately aid in boosting sales and revenue, regardless of the industry you are in. It can be challenging to persuade people to support a brand when marketing communications seem generic or uninspired. However, if the messaging is personalized and seems to have substance, trust will be built almost quickly. As a result of this strong sense of trust, greater business growth will occur than if the StoryBrand marketing structure had not been used.

Become a pioneer in your field

Your marketing efforts will become noticeably more successful when you commit to implementing the StoryBrand marketing strategy as opposed to relying on outmoded tactics. Additionally, clients will be less inclined to choose one of your rivals if you can convince them that their needs and wants are important and encourage them to buy a product or service from your company. Consequently, your business becomes the preferred choice for clients looking for high-quality goods or services that satisfy their requirements.

Increase your promotion by using customer recommendations

The StoryBrand structure was created with the intention of forming devoted customers that actively refer your company to friends and family as well as other consumers. Many businesses seek out this kind of word-of-mouth promotion since it is so valuable in today's cutthroat marketplace, especially for enterprises trying to make money.

The StoryBrand framework aims to change more than just how you promote your goods and services; it also affects how you interact with your staff and how you perceive your brand as a whole. Customers will feel as though they fully understand what makes your company tick if you have a strong brand identity and present a consistent story across all media, and this greater awareness will ultimately lead to your firm becoming nothing short of unforgettable.

There is no excuse not to attempt the StoryBrand marketing structure when there are such advantages linked with it. It only makes sense to test out the marketing strategy that has been shown to work as experimenting with various marketing tactics may be quite expensive and time-consuming.

Try out the StoryBrand marketing strategy to see how it may help your brand change, bringing in more devoted customers and boosting profits along the way.

Chapter 1:

ADVANCED STORY BRANDING

Every retail business owner has a tale to tell, whether it's about how they got started, why they chose this line of work, or how they converted a hobby into a successful enterprise. These stories intertwine to form a brand story.

There are other people who need to hear that story besides you. It strikes a chord with both your staff and customers, building a community of brand defenders who stick by and defend it.

The effectiveness of storytelling is also supported by science. Not only do our brains process stories, but also the human emotions they reflect. We are able to empathize when we comprehend the ideas and feelings of another.

This fosters genuine emotional ties that may lead to trust and, ultimately, financial success. Because of this, it's essential to learn how to create a brand story that is particular to you and your business.

If you've never thought about the history of your brand, we'll explain why it's so crucial and how you may approach it on your own. For some inspiration, we'll also give examples of retailers with compelling brand histories.

A brand story is what?

A captivating narrative explaining how and why your brand behaves the way it does is known as a brand story. It narrates the history, principles, objectives, and mission of your business.

This narrative establishes the context for all of your brand's interactions with customers, both in-person and online.

Both the personnel and the customer should understand the company's mission statement from the brand story.

The value of storytelling in branding

By establishing a connection with your audience, fostering client loyalty and trust, and differentiating your company from the competition, you may increase sales.

Connecting With Clients

The managing director of Orndee Omnimedia, a PR and brand development company, Alexandrea Merrell, emphasizes the significance of brand story. It's a crucial component of contemporary marketing, she claims. Consumers used to solely be concerned about pricing and functionality.

Consumers today consider more than just price tags and discounts.

"Consumers want to connect with a back story and ethos those appeals to their sense of self," adds

Merrell. A [retailer] must determine their target demographic and make sure they are crafting and communicating an engaging brand story.

The message that forges a strong emotional bond between your business, customers, and the broader public is known as a "story brand."

Fostering Loyalty and Trust

Even without a sizable marketing budget, great brand stories enable smaller merchants to draw in new clients and keep them coming back for more.

When done right, it creates a magical bond and develops a relationship [beyond] products, Bennett claims. If the brand story is successful, it will result in a rise in revenue as well as faster company growth and a culture that supports the brand experience.

Adding variety to your brand

Branding will either convince a customer to buy from you or from your competition, asserts Cassandra Rosen, branding expert and cofounder of FK Interactive, a brand creation and public relations firm.

Branding and narrative are what will prompt them to take a chance on your brand if they have never purchased from you before.

How to tell the tale of your brand

Now that you are aware of the significance of presenting your brand story, read on for information on how to do it. You must decide your why, comprehend your product and target market, emphasize human tales, and maintain brevity in your messaging.

Figure out why.

Always begin your brand story with the motivation behind what you do. For instance, prAna's "why" is sustainability, whereas Nordstrom's is exceptional customer service?

The following inquiries will assist you in discovering your why:

- Why are we here?
- How can we change the world for the better?
- What is the goal?
- What do we hold dear?
- What spurred me on to launch my business?

Consider the origins of your brand and the narrative that surrounds it. Take a step back and look for the purpose of [your brand] beyond products, advises Bennett suggests thinking back to your initial motivation for entering your sector as one of the initial stages in telling a brand's story. It's not necessary for your tale to be ground-breaking.

Merrell asserts that many of the most interesting brand histories began when someone set out to create a solution for a problem they were having.

Understanding the why, though, might be challenging, particularly if you established your firm solely with the intention of making money.

People don't buy so that you can make money, asserts Rosen. They are looking for anything to improve their life in some way or to find a solution to an issue they are facing personally or professionally. It is your responsibility as a retailer to choose how to accomplish this for them and to do so in a way that enhances their sense of self-worth and decision-making.

Having trouble? Merrell provides a case study for businesses that sell t-shirts. The brand story for a shop of t-shirts looking to capitalize on an internet craze may be dull, but you can provide a fresh brand narrative. The brand story Merrell recommends for that retailer of t-shirts is as follows:

I wanted to do more than just give food to my neighborhood no-kill cat shelter. I wanted to check if t-shirts with the same amusing poses and sayings would be popular after reading that videos of cats doing funny or cute things were the most popular on YouTube. To begin, I listed five t-shirt designs and informed visitors that 20% of sales would be used to help the Topeka No-Kill Cat Shelter. People did indeed react. Now, I post a total of the donations received each month on the website and share numerous images of the cat sanctuary on my social media.

That is a narrative that will inspire customers to support your brand. When people can see your passion, they want to be a part of it, adds Merrell.

Recognize your product

Understanding how and where your product fits within your brand's narrative is essential to knowing it. A brand story that is unrelated to your product may result in an enthusiastic following but little sales.

According to Conway, one of the major mistakes brands make when it comes to their narrative is lack of self-awareness in the product. Selling a Kia isn't the same as selling a Mercedes. Although they are both cars, their quality, performance, experience expectations, and price point are all different.

Conway suggests posing the following inquiries to yourself in order to determine how your product fits within your brand story:

What are the product's quality and pricing range?

Does my product make the customer feel a specific way, or does it solve a problem?

How does my product vary from those of my rivals?

Merrell provides another illustration:

There is a presumption that your pasta sauce is natural, possibly even organic, if you established your pasta sauce brand in your mother's kitchen using your grandmother's recipe and fresh vegetables from the garden. The gap between the past and the present, however, will be a problem for consumers if the contemporary version is mass-produced and loaded with additives and chemicals. There is still a chance for retailers who committed the aforementioned error to receive compensation. Use the Back to the Start commercial for Chipotle as an example. They respond to the situation and take a stand, even though they didn't actually commit the error of using ingredients from mass-produced foods, in the hopes that consumers will support them.

Recognize your audience

You must be aware of your audience if you are to create a compelling brand story. Knowing your target demographic is the third thing to keep in mind while starting your brand story. It can be easier to understand how your brand story fits into their life if you are aware of their hobbies and problems.

Conway offers the following additional considerations:

- What is at risk if a customer chooses not to purchase my product?
- Who are my current clients?
- Who is the ideal client for me?

Although defining your ideal client can be a daunting task, it's crucial for creating a brand story that will resonate. Instead of speaking directly to their target audience, many businesses attempt to appeal to all shoppers.

In targeting 'all,' [retailers] get 'few,' because very few products are everything to everybody, claims Conway.

Rosen echoes the advice to don't try to be everything to everyone, realizing that it can be difficult for smaller merchants without sizable customer bases to pinpoint the perfect client. If this is you, she advises creating a list of the beliefs you uphold and considering the kinds of clients those ideals may appeal to.

Simply comprehending and relating to your ideal customer is insufficient. In order to establish deep connections that lead to purchases, you must demonstrate your enthusiasm and embody your brand story.

People don't support the statement; I want to be the biggest T-shirt manufacturer, according to Merrell. Instead, use 'I want to offer work for 500 people and help restore and rejuvenate the community around our manufacturing facility.' People can support and participate in this cause by buying your items.

Be succinct and transparent.

There's a good chance that you know someone who struggles to communicate stories. They don't get straight to the point; instead, they ramble on about topics like when their alarm went off that morning or how many eggs they had for breakfast.

It can be challenging to communicate the stories that are closest to us. Why? Because we can become engrossed in minutiae we believe to be significant, but which may really undermine our main point.

Your brand story must be reduced and improved upon after the initial draft. Consider yourself a sculptor who begins with an unformed piece of marble. The final product becomes more distinct—and memorable—as you remove more.

Sharing your brand's history with someone who hasn't heard it before can be beneficial. They can point out sections that are unclear because you either gave too much or not enough information.

Chapter 2:

Why Most Marketing Is a Money Pit,

In the middle of the 1980s, there was a delightful film starring Tom Hanks and Shelley Long called The Money Pit about a couple who bought a property and kept finding additional problems that required them to spend money to fix. Eventually, if I recall correctly, the house just fell apart.

I've worked in sales and marketing for over 25 years, so I thought I'd offer some examples of money wasted on marketing.

£50,000 is spent annually on Yellow Pages advertisements. Putting unread brochures in skips. Pursuing the top Google spot at all costs.

Too many companies waste money on absurd marketing efforts that have no discernible return on investment. Others stop doing profitable advertisements because they get tired of them.

Our part-time marketing directors have observed innumerable instances where businesses misspend money and undermine their own initiatives. Take note of our selection of the worst below!

PPC: competing for the top Google spot

A few of the MDs I've met spend six figures annually on PPC because they need to rank first on Google. Pure pride drives their desire to outperform rivals. The MD and Google are the only people who care. They've been moved to position 2.2 or 2.4 after I sat them down, reviewed the situation, applied some clever keywords, and assisted them in chasing lower ranks. They typically receive twice as many clicks, and the spend is more than cut in half.

Take the same old, same old strategy with advertising. During my time working with one CEO, Yell was receiving almost £50,000 annually, or half of the company's yearly marketing budget. The majority of that appeared in printed Yellow Pages. Almost all advertisements were measured using Smartphone data, but the information was never analyzed. At each renewal meeting, the Yell representative did little more than provide some dubious headline figures and guesses-based assumptions, adding 5% to the cost each time.

When we completed the data analysis, we found that many of those ads had been generating no responses for years. The same folks tended to gravitate around those who were productive. The strategy was the creation of the company's founder, and the Yell representative was a friend of theirs, therefore it had never been questioned, let alone disputed. Instead of paying to re-attract customers who should have been in a database after the first sale, we advised cutting future spending on Yell advertising, adding the existing customers to a CRM and contacting them on a retention basis, switching spend to acquisitive channels, and developing content.

Are people taking notice of the promotional materials?

We always print a ton of glossy pamphlets, and in five years, 99% of them will still be around and get thrown away, said MDs. They continue to do it out of habit despite knowing it doesn't work. The worst example I've come across was a business that permanently hired someone to translate every glossy brochure they produced into eight different languages. The output of that guy filled a storehouse the size of a container. They never made another brochure, and 95% of it ended up in a skip (it actually took eight skips to get rid of everything). The printers were the only ones to voice complaints.

Brochures aren't absolutely useless, but one organization was publishing them out of habit rather than as part of a calculated, data-driven plan.

A brochure that is picked up, read, and results in a sale is still valuable; the key is to evaluate the effectiveness of your strategies and make any adjustments.

What are your employees doing with their time systems? The worst waste I've ever witnessed included a company that hired someone to devote two days a month going through their database and crossing off anybody who has unsubscribed to their emails. The Finance Director refused to pay me to update the unsubscribe when I brought it up in a meeting, to which I retorted, Why are you paying for anyone to update the unsubscribe? I gently reminded them that this would be automatically taken care of for them by a simple CRM/email marketing system. The space became silent! They've transitioned to a CRM system, which saves them time and money by automating the majority of their email marketing.

What goals do you have for your strategy? Is it priceless or not?

Small adjustments can have significant effects on a company's operations, thus it is important to consider whether future plans are worthwhile. In the middle of altering their logo because the directors had gotten tired of the previous one, our final marketing director joined a company.

"The strategy they adopted only made matters worse. The COO wanted a "D-Day" approach instead of the usual two or three months it would take to implement a change so that old stock with the current logo on it could be ran down. To recycle six pallet loads of paper, including letterheads, brochures, compliment slips, and other items, as well as to bring in the same number of rebranded stationery and brochures, we ultimately worked for 24 hours while many individuals were paid overtime. Even without accounting for the opportunity cost of lost working hours, design, material, and shipping charges alone cost the UK branch of the company £120,000.

"The worst part? The clients could not tell anything had changed. They modified the typography somewhat and went from yellow and black to white and black.

Within three months, the company left the UK, and within six, they were acquired.

There is a theme running across all of these anecdotes. The businesses involved aren't concentrating on strategies and techniques that have a demonstrated return on investment; instead, they stick with what they've always done, what everyone else is doing, or what makes sense at the time. Data, not intuition, must be the driving force behind effective marketing.

There are four techniques to ensure that your marketing is not a money waste.
There is nothing more inefficient than spending money on marketing that isn't targeted to your customer.

1. **Survey your customers and choose the correct target**. First of all, your goal is too broad, and secondly, the marketing message will also be off-target.

2. **Develop the ability to say no.** No matter what you are marketing, you will receive unsolicited bids from organizations looking for sponsorship on radio, in print, on television, and online. A well-planned campaign doesn't require unsolicited proposals because you should have already determined well in advance where you are going to focus your budget, so anything unsolicited should be answered with an outright no, no questions asked, except, in the extremely unlikely event that you have funds saved for an unforeseen chance.

3. **Have a plan**. The second tip, of course, assumes that you actually have one. Less than 20% of small and medium-sized businesses we benchmarked had a written marketing strategy, so do yourself a

favor and spend the time to create one. You'll thank yourself later for it. Every opportunity to market to clients may seem good if you don't have a plan, but with one you'll be able to tell whether it is or not.

4. **Measure Results** - After implementing any marketing program or campaign, you should assess the results, including the quantity of leads, prospects, visits, and sales that were generated. Don't do something if you can't measure it in the first place. Put the same expectations on your marketing and ensure you see a return, just like when you own a home and invest money on something: a gorgeous new garden, newly painted wall, or remodeled bathroom.

Chapter 3:

IMPLEMENTING YOUR STORY BRAND IN COMPANY SCRIPT.

Examples of StoryBrand Brand Scripts

StoryBrand the blueprints for your company's marketing communications are called BrandScripts. It has assisted well-known companies like Pantene, Intel, and charity: water in crystallizing their messages and drawing in more customers. Donald Miller, the creator of StoryBrand, introduced us to the BrandScript, which is based on the StoryBrand Framework, a road map drawn from the most famous stories ever told. This framework defines seven components that are common to all great narratives, in which your client serves as the protagonist and your brand serves as the narrator.

Corporate mission statements lack the specificity of a StoryBrand BrandScript because it tells employees everything they need to know about the company's objectives. Companies can improve their marketing communications and tell a story that connects with their target audience by using a StoryBrand BrandScript.

Due to their failure to streamline their marketing messages, the majority of businesses today perish in the sea of competition. As a result, they virtually always talk about themselves, their marketing materials look confusing, and dealing with them feels like a lot of labor.

Even if you work in the industry of building flashy websites, having a website that seems flashy and extremely high-tech won't automatically increase your customer base. Customers will go on before you can utter StoryBrand BrandScript if your message can't be understood in less than 5 seconds. Simplifying your marketing message is one effective strategy to stand out for your target market. Having a StoryBrand BrandScript makes it simpler to accomplish that.

Let's examine various StoryBrand BrandScript examples, scrutinize each section, and learn how to write one customized for your company.

Section 1:

The Character, the Hero, and Your Customer:

Every hero in a good story wants something. Your company needs to determine what your customers want or why they are calling you. Determine the desires of your hero and be sure to connect them to your offering.

Your target market can be more precisely defined thanks to this first section of the StoryBrand Framework. To appeal to everyone is one of the most absurd objectives that most businesses have. Today, there are billions of people on the earth, and it seems like there would be a very large target to strike. It's impossible to please everyone.

You may focus your brand messaging by getting to know your target market. Actually, a lot of firms fail because they have no idea to whom they are speaking. In the end, they produce a website that appears disjointed, a message that is overly generic, or social media updates that are incredibly simple to ignore.

Start by figuring out what they want because your story and your customer's story are not the same. Do not presume that they share your views. Do not forget that you are there to assist them, not the other way around.

Ask inquiries to learn their desires:

What would make their lives more convenient?

How could we make X better? (X is anything you provide.)

There are numerous solutions that all lead in the same direction, so compile these options and arrange them into a coherent narrative. The responses you come up with can be turned into brief but powerful messages that will draw them to your website right away.

Who inspires you? What is his goal?

Your clients are the protagonists of their own narratives. You must understand what they desire in order to assist them in improving their storytelling. Create a clear statement about how your product or service can satisfy that need using this knowledge.

Examples include the following if you are an interior designer:

My customers want to feel more at home in their surroundings. They desire to reside in a setting that embodies their concept of home.

If you represent a marketing firm, you may state:

- Our clients want to reach a wider audience and make their goods and services known to those who are in need of them.
- If your company is a nonprofit, you can say:
- Every individual on the earth needs access to clean, safe water, and we want to help.

This final illustration is taken directly from charity: water's website, an organization that employs StoryBrand Certified Guides to spread its message. Any size company or organization can utilize the StoryBrand Framework. It can support the growth of companies like yours

Section 2:

The Client's Issue:

It's time to introduce some danger into the mix now that you've established who your character is in the narrative and what they want. Describe the issue that they have. The problem is one of the seven components of a success story and is also one of the most basic. It's one of the factors that make up your brand.

All of the StoryBrand BrandScript examples you'll see in this post revolve around developing a tale that is so engaging that it truly attracts attention and demonstrates how to understand your potential clients so well that you can provide them with exactly what they need. But what are such individuals actually seeking?

You're not simply offering a product or service; you're also solving issues. Additionally, being aware of the specifics of your clients' issues provides you the ability to change your brand story so that it becomes attractive.

Every great narrative contains a certain amount of danger. Middle Earth is essentially...doomed if Frodo can't get the ring to Mount Doom! Danny

LaRusso will always feel like a loser if he can't defeat his bullies with amazing karate moves.

When your customers are aware that you comprehend what they're going through, they are more likely to trust your company. And every character in every story experiences three different kinds of issues.

To learn more about these kinds of issues, let's examine some StoryBrand BrandScript instances.

External Issue

What prevents your clients from achieving their goals?

My marketing tactics aren't yielding the steady outcomes I'm hoping for.

Even if I am selling the most beautifully designed and decorated home, no one seems to notice my listing.

I've wasted a lot of time and money on ineffective products because I want to appear younger.

Internal Issue

How do they feel about the issue outside of themselves?

Wasting time and money on inefficient marketing is really annoying.

"Moving into a new home and selling my previous house at the same time makes me feel anxious."

The lines and wrinkles steal my confidence. I feel out of sorts and believe it's my fault.

Philosophy-related Issue

Why is it wrong that these issues are a burden for your clients?

With all of the technology that is accessible to everyone today, marketing ought to be simple.

"Your home represents a significant time, financial, and emotional investment. It's wrong to sell it for less than its best value.

Living a happy and productive life shouldn't be impeded by aging, hormones, or lifestyle decisions.

You can only build a brand that will position you as the leader by responding to these three questions.

Show your clients that you have a thorough understanding of who your target market is, why their issues are important, and how your brand can provide them with what they require to live happier lives and succeed. Create a message that conveys authority and empathy while also outlining how you can assist them in succeeding because you have done it before. In the section that follows, we'll become more specific.

Similarity 7%

Examples: You May Utilize In Your Enterprise...

Apr 17, 2023 · I've wasted a lot of time and money on products that don't work, but I want to look at the younger Internal Issue. Regarding their external issue, what is their attitude? Wasting time and money on inefficient marketing is really annoying.. Moving into a new home and selling my previous house at the same time makes me feel anxious.

Section 3:

The Instructions.

Your company serves as the story's protagonist. Your customer, the main character, needs to choose the correct brand to get them to the light at the end of the tunnel in order to succeed.

It was Yoda and Ben Kenobi for Luke Skywalker. Sam was available to Frodo. Mr. Miyagi was with Danny LaRusso.

Your company's role is to demonstrate sympathy for your customers' concerns. Only someone who comprehends their situation can they trust.

You must provide an answer to the query "How do I demonstrate empathy for my clients?" in this section.

Your clients are searching for a trustworthy individual as well. You must therefore establish your authority. Take a look at these instances of StoryBrand BrandScript from actual businesses.

Understanding:

- We understand how frustrating it's when you do n't getting the anticipated lift you need from your marketing creative when you need it.
- We believe each home is truly special and deserves a customized marketing plan that helps buyers fete its oneness.
- We understand how frustrating performance problems, stubborn fat, and growing skin can be.

Credibility

- By applying the proven principles of behavioral wisdom to your marketing, you can produce constantly effective marketing strategies that drive guests to act with confidence.
- Our moxie in the prevailing original request, as well as our gift for staging and preparing homes, showcases your property's true implicitness and launches your home onto the request.
- We've made innumerous men and women feel and look stylish.

Section 4

The Strategy

Simply said, this part describes how simple it's for your guests to conduct business with you.

Up to three phases that outline how guests should do are advised by StoryBrand.

Illustration 1: Three easy ways to ameliorate your marketing impact right now

1. View some educational vids

2. Choose the package that stylish meets your company's requirements.

3. Get reliable issues from your Marketing

Chapter 4:

DETERMINING YOUR CONSUMERS' PROBLEMS

Humans naturally have a negative bias, which causes us to notice negative stimuli more quickly and to concentrate on those events more frequently. Customers and their pain spots are subject to the same issue.

Sales representatives enquiring about customer business problems

Customers are more likely to make a purchase decision if they believe your solution may ease the discomfort of their ongoing pain points, even though it is crucial to discuss all the advantages and amazing characteristics of your product.

You may develop a more persuasive plan that will elevate your firm in the eyes of your clients' by recognizing and resolving their pain areas in your marketing and sales activities.

What are the causes of pain?

A product or service's pain points are ongoing issues that can annoy customers and their businesses. Or, to put it more simply, they are unfulfilled wants that are just waiting to be met.

A product or service's pain points are ongoing issues that can annoy customers and their businesses. Or, to put it another way, they are needs that must be satisfied but have not yet been supplied.

Customers may experience physical, emotional, or logistical discomfort that is tied to their personal or work lives.

Some potential customers might not even be aware of the problems they have. You need to persuade them that there is a problem and that your business has the answer to remedy it.

Understanding Customer Pain Points

We are aware that clients and prospects experience pain points, but how can you find them?

To understand the nature of your customers' pain points, perform qualitative research. Pain points can be as varied and distinct as the people who experience them. Then you'll be able to see how you fit into fixing them.

The following steps will help you identify those pain locations.

Locating the pain points. Engage your audience. Query your sales staff. Review customer comments.

Step1. Interact with the audience.

Allowing your customers to directly communicate with you is the best method to learn about their problems. Conduct customer research using tools including interviews, focus groups, and surveys.

You can better comprehend and address consumer issues by posing focused inquiries and paying close attention to the responses. Additionally, you ought to add a live chat feature to your website so that visitors may ask you questions and report problems.

Step 2. Consult your sales staff.

The sales team at your organization regularly communicates with clients and potential clients. They are an invaluable resource for learning about the ongoing problems that your clients are experiencing and how you can help.

Additionally, your sales team will have a unique viewpoint on client pain issues that can assist you in identifying underlying patterns and even pain concerns that some consumers are unaware of.

However, if your sales staff is having trouble completing deals, you should be cautious to make sure you are distinguishing between consumer pain points and pain points your sales team may be experiencing.

Step 3. Examine client comments.

Most likely, your current and potential clients are expressing their complaints online. You may turn those uncomfortable spots into effective selling points for your company if you know where to search.

Analyze your customer service tickets to discover the problems that your clients are experiencing, and keep an eye out on social media and online reviews to discover the problems that others in your sector are encountering. To assist with this endeavor, think about using social listening tools.

In this book, I'll break down more particular circumstances, but to get you started, here are a few common types of pain points you might experience.

- A customer requires a service that is more expensive.
- Financial constraints prevent clients from functioning effectively, which causes them to look for more economical solutions.

- A company having an overly complicated strategy.
- A need to shorten process lead time is shown when it is too long and costs money.
- Departmental communication is lacking.

To cut down on errors during the process, teams must figure out how to share information effectively.

These are all circumstances that "pain" or impede productivity. Let's talk about how to do it for your consumers since it is the first step in alleviating these pains.

Taking Care of Customer Pain Points

Your customers can fill you in on everything, from complaints about poor customer service to dissatisfaction with a good or service to suggestions for new innovations that you haven't yet thought of.

There are numerous techniques for locating and addressing client pain points.

Listening to what they have to say is the wisest course of action.

Your main source of income is customers. They are a top priority, regardless of whether they buy a finished good or a support service to carry out their business. So let's move on to what it means for a firm to have pain points.

Business Pain Points

Business pain points are issues that an organization experiences and for which you have a remedy. Real business suffering does not have a problem with a nice-to-have remedy. It's the kind of issue that must be resolved, is funded, and is considered at the board level.

Businesses must address them if they want to succeed since they have an impact on the bottom line. Business problems must be resolved immediately because they prevent the company from operating.

Examples of Business Pain Points

There are many more problems that have a negative impact on a company's bottom line, which are referred to as business pain points.

Top salespeople look for pain in their prospects first since it triggers the buyer's journey to locate a solution in potential clients.

The most typical categories of business pain points, along with samples of each, that your prospects might be experiencing are listed below.

Types of pain points in business.

- Businesses that want to place themselves in the market experience positioning discomfort, or difficulties.

- Financial difficulties are problems brought on by money.
- Problems with morale, turnover, people management, and culture are examples of people's suffering.
- Process pain refers to difficulties in repeatable process implementation in the business.
- Roadblocks that impede a business and its people from operating effectively are known as productivity pain. Small-business pain: difficulties that are unique to small enterprises

Identifying Pain Point Locations

The difficulties companies confront while trying to place themselves in the market are referred to as positioning pain. These problems might appear when companies find it difficult to set themselves apart from rivals or to attract and engage their target audience.

Examples of things you might hear from prospects that are having positioning issues are as follows:

1. Nobody is familiar with our business.

The market is shifting, leaving us behind, and our rivals are spending more money than we are.Our competition has more green space on most channels because we haven't thought about digital marketing up until now, which puts us behind.

Assume you can see potential clients who are struggling with positioning and provide them with advice on how to carve out a niche and gain customers' attention. In that situation, they will undoubtedly find you're good or service to be useful.

2. Financial Problems

In business, money is everything. It's a problem when you don't have enough of it, and most problems are easier when you do. Every business gains from raising its financial position.

Here are some instances of financial problems that demand significant solutions:

- Not enough is being sold for us to keep the lights on.
- Although sales are growing, profitability is poor.
- We lack sufficient transparency to determine whether our financial decisions are sound.

- We may be paying too much for the tools and equipment, but we are unsure of where to make cuts.
- Emphasizing your reduced price point (if applicable) will be beneficial when working with prospects that are suffering financial difficulties. You might succeed with prospects experiencing this kind of business suffering if your solutions can manage cash flow and cut expenses.

3. Individual Pain Points

Every firm is centered around its people, who are frequently both its biggest expense and best asset.

Problems in other company areas may arise if there are personnel concerns like the ones listed below:

- Low morale among employees."We lose our best employees to higher paying positions elsewhere."
- Lack of innovation is a result of our lack of variety.
- We can't rely on our middle managers to develop and inspire employees.
- What we declared and our actual corporate culture are not the same.
- If your product or service makes managing, rewarding, or delighting staff easier for

businesses, you'll be a hero and the sale will be sealed.

4. Process Problems

Operational issues often accompany problems with the people involved (or vice versa). Your target audience is aware that using repeatable processes is the greatest method to achieve consistent success. The issue is: "How?"

They could be struggling with obstacles like:

- We have a cumbersome hiring procedure and have trouble locating applicants who are highly competent.
- Since our service crew is overworked and unable to keep up, customer churn is significant.
- There is no mechanism in place for qualifying leads for us.
- The software we use is antiquated, but we worry that switching to a new one will be challenging. Each employee's workflow is inconsistent, which results in disorganization and uneven performance.
- Ask your prospect to imagine what a smoothly operating business, division, or system would feel like and what type of difference it would make if you discover process pain points.

5. Productivity Hurdles

It is a manager's responsibility to eliminate obstacles from the team's path so that work gets done, productivity stays high, and revenues rise. Having said that, it's simple to become bogged down in the minutiae of the business and succumb to time-wasting inefficiencies.

Here are some instances of productivity issues in the workplace:

- We frequently miss deadlines with clients.
- Our administrative work is out of control, and we spend far too much time in meetings.
- Costly recalls and customer turnover have resulted from quality problems with our goods.
- Our staff don't receive adequate support to finish the duties they've been given.
- You can present your solution as a time, money, and headache saver if something prevents a company and its people from functioning effectively.

6. Problems Small Businesses Face

When problems in a small business are not resolved, the business may cease to exist.

In contrast to a giant organization where workers don't need to wear as many hats, if your customer is a small business, you need to ask questions addressing the numerous jobs a small team must do

The following are some instances of small business pain points:

- Orders frequently arrive after they should, and our staff is already under a lot of pressure to keep up.
- Finding the greatest talent for the company hasn't been simple.
- It takes time to post on all of our social media platforms.
- Since I already have a lot of responsibilities at my company, leading a team is scary.
- As time goes on, accounting becomes harder to keep up with.

With a product or service offering based on modern technology and consultation, many of these problems can be solved. Workflow automation and correct coaching from seasoned experts could be helpful to small organizations.

4 Strategies for Dealing with Business Pain

You can work out a solution for your prospect's problem once you've identified their pain. Business pain points are a fantastic resource for salespeople to use. Instead of selling products, you may start a business providing solutions.

Here are four pointers to help you begin assuming this position.

How to Handle Pain in a Business.

When discussing suffering, use the language your prospect would use. Find out who has the authority to end the suffering. Decide on extra important stakeholders as soon as you can. Your offer should be framed to address the prospect's concern.

1. When describing suffering to your prospect, speak in their language.

This psychological tactic can significantly help you win your prospect's trust. Show your prospect you take them seriously by speaking to them on an equal footing and use their language and vocabulary, as opposed to trying to sound impressive by relying on jargon only your colleagues would understand.

2. Determine who has the authority to ease the suffering.

Locate the economic buyer as soon as you can. Ask your potential customer whose budget the purchase would come from and which teams would be involved in the decision to make the purchase.

Spending hours with someone who is unable to close a deal is pointless.

3. Establish additional important stakeholders as soon as you can.

You need to be aware right away if you're marketing to many teams and one team has entirely different priorities than another. If you have to go through a two-month legal review procedure before you can consummate a contract, you also need to know in advance.

I like to utilize the following questions to avoid the impression that prospects are less authoritative if they admit that they are not the only decision-maker:

- Who else needs to be involved in this decision other than you?
- Who else might be interested in knowing that we had this discussion?

4. Present your proposal with the prospect's predicament in mind.

You must tailor the solution to the prospect's unique needs as you gain their trust and pay attention to varied viewpoints. For instance, if your product has several uses, explain which characteristics will help customers with their difficulties.

When requesting information from a prospect, pay attention and validate their problems. Making your pitch fit everyone's needs will be simpler.

Recognizing Pain Points

Empathy is key to inbound sales. Start asking the proper questions to the right prospects in order to close more business and be as helpful as you can. You'll soon be aware of their greatest difficulties and how you may help.

Chapter 5:

TAKING ON THE ROLE OF THE GUIDE

The Best Way to Fit Yourself Into Your Customer's Story

The finest sales strategy involves using stories.

People adore stories, especially those that are captivating, memorable, and interesting. Because they transform their sales pitch from an informational seminar to an engaging event that their potential clients appreciate, those who sell with stories are extremely successful.

Donald Miller, the founder and CEO of StoryBrand, is a pioneer in the field of selling with narrative in addition to being an expert in it. The StoryBrand approach succeeds because it appeals to clients in so many ways, from entertainment to comprehension to even survival, as he recently covered in his Digital Marketer class. The same outcome occurs in each of these various ways: Your buyer actually pays attention to what you have to say.

They are more likely to pay attention when you write a tale about them, especially if they are the protagonist. They often respond. Most significantly, they frequently make purchases.

The storytellers all have the same issue with this strategy, and it can be summed up in one straightforward query.

Where do I fit into all of this?

Unquestionably, the protagonist and main character of the narrative is your customer. You must draw attention to the narrative arc that shows them overcoming challenges and achieving their objectives. But how should you position yourself if they are the protagonist of the tale?

What part do you play in the narrative?

- You serve as the narrator in your customer's story.
- The guide is the one who assists the main character in overcoming obstacles. Like Yoda, Dumbledore, and Mr. Miyagi, they are fictional figures. They are the ones who are cherished in memory, not the ones who triumphantly raise their arms at the conclusion of the book or film.

In practically every story, the guide plays a crucial part because they are the ones who enable the hero's change. The guide is essential to the hero's ability to overcome challenges and accomplish their objectives. Your consumer won't be able to accomplish their goals without your products and experience, much as Luke Skywalker wouldn't be able to fight the Sith without Yoda's assistance.

Therefore, despite the fact that you are essential to the plot, you are not the protagonist. And it's crucial to keep that in mind while crafting your customer's story for a few reasons:

Because the hero is the one who is ill-equipped to accomplish their objectives on their own, you should never assume the role of the hero. They won't be able to achieve greatness until the guide appears and provides them with the necessary resources. You want to be the one that helps the main character ultimately succeed, not the one who can't seem to manage to accomplish their goals on their own.

The impact of a tale on your audience is diminished when there are two heroes, which is the second reason you shouldn't utilize them. When two protagonists and two narrative arcs are introduced, the stories of you and your customers diverge drastically (and become confusing).

Therefore, even though you want to succeed, you depend even more on your customer. Invite your audience to participate in a tale in which a character overcomes all odds to triumph. Discuss the ambitions and desires of your consumer, not your own. In all you do, prioritize serving your customers.

After your customer has grasped this and started down the road to success, you will also succeed in the process. Don't concentrate on your personal needs and wants. Simply assist others, then take a back seat and observe how things come together.

You won't ever have to worry about your own success if you can pull that off. It will just happen naturally.

How to Make Yourself Known as the Leader

You must now learn how to play the role you have been assigned after having determined what it is. We spoke generally about it, so let's go more concrete.

You must demonstrate that you are the one who can assist your client in achieving their goals if you want to be taken seriously as the advisor. You need to act with authority and empathy to accomplish it.

When it comes to empathy, you need to demonstrate to your client that you genuinely care. You need to let them know that you not only feel awful that they are experiencing an issue with their business, but that you also believe it is unjust of them to have to go through it in the first place. Customers are far more likely to let you help them repair a problem if you can demonstrate that you genuinely care about their issue (and assisting them in solving it).

You fundamentally need to show that you are competent when it comes to authority. You must demonstrate that this isn't the first time you've assisted a client in resolving an issue and achieving their objectives. You can persuade a customer that you are the best person to help them with their problems by demonstrating your ability to do so and your track record of success. You're going to build the crucial foundation of any commercial connection, which is trust.

How to write your brand script

The two components of the equation when it comes to your particular function as the narrator in your brand "script" are empathy and authority. It's also crucial to keep in mind that they are not mutually exclusive. Your entire positioning strategy will fail if you can only develop one of empathy or authority.

When speaking to your customer, you should try to create authority and empathy in no more than one or two phrases. You'll achieve tremendous success if you can do each of those things in a timely manner.

That truly means that you need to make plans in advance. You should make an effort to foresee the type of issue your consumer will encounter. By doing this, you can incorporate the basic structure of your statement of authority and empathy into your brand script and then add the details as you learn them.

Once you've made that remark loud and clear, you'll have successfully established the framework for assuming the role of the guide. After that, you may concentrate on ensuring that the remaining components of your customer's tale come together. The remaining parts of your brand narrative are your responsibility.

No matter how crucial it may be, always keep in mind that your role in your customer's narrative is just one piece of a much larger puzzle. Visit Donald Miller's workshop if you want to find out more about the StoryBrand procedure and how to complete your customer story.

Wrap-Up

By assuming the role of the guide in their success narrative, you contribute significantly to their achievement without taking away from the fact that it is their success, not yours. The ideal technique to convince your client that you are not just competent but also caring is by demonstrating to them that they can depend on you in times of need so that you can assist them in finding solutions.

Once they do, you'll be able to effectively assist them in realizing their personal achievement goals. Additionally, you will be compensated during the process. Once your client is content and their tale has been completed, you may move on to the next client and continue the procedure. What is superior to that?

Chapter 6:

INVOLVING YOUR CLIENT

New customer acquisition is frequently seen by business owners and managers as one of their top priorities. However, maintaining current clients through efficient engagement tactics is also crucial. Building great relationships with your clients and attending to their needs can help you keep them satisfied and ultimately bring in new business.

In this book, I will address customer involvement and provide 11 strategies for forging genuine and fruitful connections.

Key conclusions:

Customer engagement is the practice of interacting with customers across a variety of channels in order to improve customer relationships, boost customer retention rates, and foster increased brand loyalty.

Effective customer involvement may result in enhanced brand recognition, more recommendations and referrals, higher revenue, and a devoted customer base.

You may improve your customer engagement process by paying attention to customer feedback, gathering data, rewarding engagement, and reengaging clients, among other things.

What is Customer engagement:?

The process of communicating with a company's audience through a variety of channels and strengthening the relationship with them is known as customer engagement. Any interaction a business has with a customer during that customer's relationship with the brand is referred to as customer engagement. Customer engagement for the majority of businesses starts with the initial customer interaction and continues even after the consumer makes a purchase of a good or service.

One of the key factors in individuals choosing to purchase from particular businesses is a satisfying customer experience. Customer engagement has several advantages.

- Enduring, strong connections
- Greater brand awareness
- A competitive advantage over rivals
- Referrals and recommendations
- Positive ratings and comments
- Devoted clientele
- A rise in sales
- Resolve customer complaints immediately and accept responsibility for errors to increase clients' faith in your business.

How to interact with clients

Your business may address client wants and broaden its audience by engaging with customers. The following list of 11 efficient client involvement techniques:

1. Increase your social media activity,

2. Encourage participation

3. Share reviews.

4. Pay attention to criticism;

5. Gather and use data;

6. Keep your word

7. Provide a product manual

8. Request suggestions

9. Send emails of gratitude

10. Hold occasions

11. Re-engage your audience

Increase your social media presence

Companies can communicate with both present and potential customers through social media in a variety of ways. Businesses may utilize social media to:

- Declare discounts and sales
- Share specials of the day
- Display fresh items

Display adjustments made to their product lines or stores

Nowadays, many businesses prefer social media to their websites for client interaction. Customers can follow their preferred brands, goods, or services on social media networks, and they can receive notifications when new content is posted.

The "tag a friend" tactic is one technique to use social media to interact with customers and expand your audience. To be eligible for a contest, ask your fans to tag their friends in the comments section of one of your posts. If your page's content appeals to them and they receive notices that they have been tagged, they may decide to follow you as well.

Encourage participation

Engage with current and potential consumers on several channels to develop a reputation for being helpful and responsive. You can find communication tools that let you organize all of your customer involvement channels while managing many accounts.

Your most loyal clients may spread good word about your business and goods if you reward them.

As an illustration, you might provide your devoted consumers freebies, discounts, or loyalty program points. A person of your team should be given the responsibility of identifying and rewarding customers who post about their experiences with you on social media and other websites. With this tactic, referrals come easily, quickly, and cheaply.

Advice: Engaged customers are those who are engaged with your company in some way, such as liking social media postings or clicking on marketing texts.

Share reviews.

Take a screenshot of your positive online reviews and post them on social media (don't forget to tag and thank the reviewers for their kind words). By doing this, you can draw potential customers from other customer engagement channels as well as your present clients. Additionally, it can inspire your consumers to tag others, generating more leads for your company.

Pay attention to criticism.

When interacting with people, pay attention to consumer feedback to:

- Increase the quality of your offerings
- up your client service
- Review your business operations.
- Expand your company

By attending to their requirements, you can increase consumer loyalty and build brand trust. Customers can get the impression that you appreciate their thoughts and business just by reading and reacting to their comments and suggestions.

Gather and use data

Companies that want to interact with their clients should routinely gather information about their issues and preferences. Utilize tools like surveys and questionnaires to get data that will help your organization grow. You may create powerful customer engagement strategies using this data.

You may use the data, for instance, to determine what time of day or what day of the week the majority of customers make purchases. Send them marketing communications when they are most likely to make purchases.

The following are some important metrics you may use to gauge consumer engagement:

Website statistics include things like the average amount of time a visitor spends on a page or your website overall.

Today, social media is the main channel via which businesses and brands interact with their consumers. Your consumer engagement rates might increase as you receive more likes, comments, mentions, and views on your social media channels.

On channels like email and other types of push notifications, click-through rates can be employed.

Your audience is more likely to respond to your engagement attempts the greater your click-through rate is.

Data on customers and visitors can be collected via online feedback forms. Customer retention is likely to be higher the more forms that are filled out.

Tip: High sales conversion rates and a low website bounce rate are two more crucial data metrics that can be used to gauge client involvement.

Keep your word

Make sure you can deliver on promises you make to customers, such as fixing an issue, delivering a promotion, or releasing a new product. Maintaining your word encourages consumer loyalty and trust, which can lead to glowing testimonials and recommendations.

Provide a product manual

Give clients usage instructions if your company sells complicated goods like computers, kitchen appliances, phones, or automobiles. Giving product guides to potential consumers might also provide you the chance to highlight other goods and services you provide that they might find useful.

Request suggestions

A successful customer engagement strategy is referral marketing. When customers receive recommendations from friends or family, they are more inclined to buy things from your business. Encourage customers to tell others about your brand or to recommend your company after they make a purchase. Provide rewards, like discounts or coupon cards, for each referral they make.

Send emails of gratitude

Sending emails to your consumers with thank-you messages for supporting your business or being devoted clients is a great way to show them you care. This straightforward action can enhance client relations, demonstrate your appreciation for their business, and encourage them to make additional purchases from your firm.

Hold occasions

Create a virtual event, a webinar, or a local meetup to let your clients feel like they are a part of your company's community. Look for chances to interact with your customers at other events.

You could go to industry trade exhibitions, for instance, and engage in meaningful dialogue with possible clients there. These are beneficial chances to interact with individuals and spread brand awareness.

Re-engage your audience

Find the past clients who have not recently engaged with or purchased from your business and get in touch with them. As you express gratitude for their patronage, enquire if they have any questions or comments you can address. They might be touched by your kindness and feel valued by your business. Re-engaging with dormant consumers via emails or texts might thaw the relationship and persuade them to purchase your goods or services.

Chapter 7:

Essential Metrics for Brand Storytelling: Assessing Achievement

1. The Power of Brand Storytelling Metrics

In the present digital era, when advertisements and marketing messages are constantly bombarding consumers, brands need to stand out from the competition and forge closer ties with their target market. This is where the value of brand storytelling lies. By presenting compelling stories, brands may build strong emotional bonds and long-lasting relationships with customers. However, evaluating the success of brand storytelling can be challenging. This is where brand storytelling metrics come into play; they help you make data-driven decisions that will optimize your brand's storytelling approach by providing relevant information about how effectively your storytelling activities are performing.

2. The Importance of Metrics for Brand Storytelling

Brand narrative metrics are important for several reasons. They first enable you to evaluate whether your messages are being understood by your intended audience and how effectively your storytelling is reaching them. You may track metrics like social media shares, time spent on content, and engagement rates to assess how well your brand storytelling initiatives are working.

Consider a scenario in which you have launched a video campaign detailing a customer's success in overcoming a challenge with the aid of your product. It is possible to examine metrics such as views, comments, and shares to determine whether the video was effective in holding viewers' attention and eliciting a positive response.

Secondly, metrics about brand storytelling provide valuable insights into the inclinations and actions of customers. By improving the way you tell stories and researching the kind of material that resonates best with your audience, you may increase the relevance and efficacy of your communications.

For instance, by keeping an eye on metrics like click-through and conversion rates, you may ascertain what kinds of stories elicit the most customer behaviors. With the help of this data, you might create more effective ads and enhance your narrative approach.

3. Crucial Measures to Assess Brand Storytelling's Success

You should consider several significant factors when evaluating the success of your brand storytelling campaigns.

Here are a couple of such examples:

A) Engagement metrics track how well your narrative content captivates and maintains the attention of your viewers. You can tell if your stories are engaging enough for readers to stay on them by looking at metrics like bounce rate, average time spent on a page, and scroll depth.

B) Metrics from social media platforms: By making use of the wealth of information these websites provide, you may assess the effectiveness of your brand narrative. Metrics like likes, comments, shares, and follower growth indicate how much engagement and reach your content is getting.

C) Conversion Metrics: The degree to which your brand storytelling inspires customers to act is what determines its final efficacy. Conversion metrics like click-through rates, lead generation, and purchases indicate how well your storytelling is accomplishing its goals.

4. Tips for accurately measuring brand storytelling

To ensure accurate and informative measurement of your brand storytelling initiatives, take into consideration the following advice:

1) **Clearly articulate the goals and purposes of your narrative**: Before focusing on KPIs, establish clear goals for your brand storytelling initiatives. Are you aiming to increase brand exposure, increase revenue, or forge emotional connections? Well-defined objectives will serve as the basis for your measuring strategy.

2) **Match metrics to your objectives for storytelling**: Select metrics that support the goals you have for your storytelling. For example, if increasing brand recognition is your goal, measurements like reach and

impressions may be more significant than conversion analytics.

3) **Regularly monitor and evaluate data**: Pay attention to your narrative metrics and evaluate the information to identify trends, patterns, and problem areas. Regularly reviewing your statistics can help you make data-driven decisions and maximize your narrative approach.

4. **Case Studies**: Real-World Examples of Successful Brand Storytelling Assessment

To have a better understanding of the effectiveness of brand storytelling metrics, let's look at two real-world case studies:

Case Study No. 1. Nike's Dream Crazy campaign.

The "DreamCrazy" Nike ad featuring Colin Kaepernick generated a lot of attention and conversations about social issues. Nike monitored sentiment research, video views, and social media interaction to determine the campaign's impact on sales and brand image.

Case Study 2: Airbnb's "Live There" Campaign

Airbnb's "Live There" marketing aimed to 2. What Should Be Measured and Why?

1. **Engagement metrics**: Engagement metrics are crucial for determining how well your brand storytelling efforts are reaching your target audience. These metrics help you understand the level of contact and engagement that your audience has with the content that your brand produces. Click-through rates,

likes, shares, and comments are a few crucial engagement metrics that need to be monitored. You may gauge how well your narrative is capturing the attention of your audience by keeping track of the shares and comments on your blog posts or social media material, for example.

2. **Reach Metrics**: These show how many people your message is reaching and how far your brand is taking its storytelling. These metrics let you assess the effectiveness of your distribution channels and the overall visibility of your brand's story. Reach metrics include things like website traffic, social media followers, and email open rates. By keeping an eye on these metrics, you can ascertain which channels are producing the most reach and adjust your storytelling strategies accordingly.

3. **Conversion Metrics**: These are essential for determining how well your brand narrative inspires the necessary behaviors in your target audience. These metrics show you whether or not your storytelling efforts are converting viewers into customers or subscribers. Conversion metrics include things like lead generation, purchases, email sign-ups, and downloads. For instance, if your business effectively influences visitors to take action by using a landing page to tell a compelling story and has a high lead generation rate, this indicates that your storytelling is working.

4. **Brand Perception Analytics**: Following up on your storytelling endeavors, brand perception analytics provide you with a better understanding of how your target market perceives your company. These indicators tell you whether the story of your brand is aligned with your fundamental principles and how well it resonates with your target audience. Some examples of brand perception metrics are sentiment analysis, customer surveys, and brand sentiment on social media. By monitoring this data, you may identify areas for improvement and adjust your storytelling strategy to better reflect the opinions of your audience.

5. **Metrics for Return on Investment (ROI):** To evaluate the overall effectiveness of your brand storytelling initiatives, ROI measures are crucial. These metrics allow you to analyze the financial impact of your storytelling initiatives and determine whether your investments are paying off. ROI metrics include things like revenue from narrative marketing, cost per acquisition, and customer lifetime value. By looking at ROI indicators, you may assess the success of your storytelling efforts and modify your strategy.

Ensure your storytelling goals align with the monitored data at your analytics accurately reflect the effectiveness of your brand storytelling initiatives by taking this action.

- Integrate qualitative and quantitative data to get a complete picture of your brand's narrative performance.

- Pay careful attention to your analytics and perform routine analysis to identify patterns, trends, and areas that require improvement in your narrative approach.
- To gain a better knowledge of your brand's performance and identify areas for development, compare your statistics with that of the industry or your competitors.

Case Study:

One effective example of brand storytelling metrics is the Coca-Cola "Share a Coke" campaign, which swapped out the Coke logo on bottles with well-known names to create a more intimate relationship with consumers. Coca-Cola examined social media mentions, likes, and shares to measure engagement metrics, and these data climbed dramatically across the campaign. Reach metrics such as higher sales and website traffic were employed to demonstrate increased exposure and reach. Conversion metrics were measured by sales and the number of personalized bottles that were ordered. Since positive brand perception metrics increased buyers' emotional connection to the brand, they proved the campaign's efficacy. Finally, Coca-Cola computed ROI measures by comparing the campaign's cost to the increase in sales to demonstrate a good return on investment. You may improve your brand's storytelling performance and gain valuable insights into the effectiveness of your storytelling tactics by understanding and assessing these critical brand storytelling metrics.

3. Evaluating Brand Narratives' Impact

To truly understand the impact of brand storytelling, it is imperative to measure its reach and impressions. These metrics provide valuable information about how many people have heard your brand story and how deeply it has resonated with them. Reach and impressions analysis allows you to evaluate the performance of your storytelling efforts and make informed decisions to improve the narrative of your business.

1. **Reach**: The total amounts of people who have heard your brand story is what we call reach. It helps you estimate the number of your audience and determines the degree of brand visibility. Reach can be measured across a wide range of platforms, including social media, email marketing, website analytics, and traditional media. For example, reach on social media is determined by the number of users who follow, like, share, and comment on your company's content. By tracking reach, you can decide which channels are best for telling your brand's narrative and focus resources there.

2. **Impressions**: On the other hand, impressions keep tabs on how often individuals have heard or seen your brand's narrative. It provides you with data on the frequency with which members of your audience have encountered your tale. Impressions can be measured

using a range of touch points, such as website visits, ad impressions, and video views. For instance, ad-serving platforms monitor the frequency at which advertisements are displayed to track impressions in digital advertising. By looking at impressions, you can assess how much exposure your brand narrative has had and discover methods to enhance its delivery.

Suggestion:

- Use analytics tools: Use Google Analytics, social media insights, and advertising platforms, among other analytics tools, to precisely track reach and impressions. These sites provide comprehensive data that can help you assess the success of your brand storytelling campaigns.

- Create benchmarks: Set benchmarks for reach and impressions based on previous campaigns and industry standards. This will enable you to identify areas that require improvement and assess the success of your brand storytelling efforts.

- Consider engagement metrics: Measuring reach and impressions is not nearly as important as analyzing engagement indicators such as likes, comments, shares, and click-through rates. These metrics let you know how well your brand narrative is engaging your target audience and fostering strong bonds.

A Case Study of Nike's "Dream Crazy" Campaign

The "Dream Crazy" Nike commercial starring Colin Kaepernick received a lot of attention and impressions. The program, which aimed to empower and inspire athletes, sparked conversations everywhere. Nike's social media posts garnered millions of likes, shares, and comments, resulting in a large following. Millions of people watched the campaign's TV commercial, which attracted a lot of media attention. Nike tracked the reach and impressions of the campaign to assess its effectiveness and gauge how well its story was told.

In summary, measuring impressions and reach is critical to determining how successful brand storytelling is. These metrics assist you in making fact-based, well-informed decisions by providing you with data on how your brand story is perceived and distributed. By keeping an eye on impressions and reach, setting targets, and considering engagement metrics, you can enhance and boost the efficacy of your brand storytelling efforts.

4. From Story to Advertising

One of the key goals of brand storytelling is to increase sales and convert more customers. While producing engrossing stories that resonate with your audience is important, it's also crucial to keep an eye on the analytics to see if your efforts are translating into revenue. Consider the following crucial conversion indicators when evaluating the impact of your brand narrative:

1. **Conversion Rate**: This is arguably the simplest number to keep an eye on. It determines the percentage of users who finish a desired task, like making a purchase, filling out a form, or subscribing to a newsletter. You can utilize your conversion rate to gauge how well your storytelling is leading to quantifiable results.

For example, suppose you launched a brand storytelling campaign on your website featuring engaging videos that showcase the unique features of your offering. By keeping an eye on the conversion rate, you may determine whether the films are successfully converting visitors into customers. If, after the campaign, the conversion rate increases, it is clear that your story is resonating with and impacting purchases from your intended audience.

Suggestion: To improve your conversion rate, consider customizing your narrative content to fit certain conversion goals. For example, if you want to increase sales, include compelling calls-to-action in your brand story to persuade readers to buy something.

2. **Average Order Value (AOV)**: This measure reveals the average amount a customer spends on each purchase. By keeping an eye on the AOV, you may ascertain whether your brand narrative efforts are effectively up selling or cross-selling to customers.

For example, suppose the objective of your brand storytelling campaign is to emphasize the variety and compatibility of your products. By comparing the average order value (AOV) before and after the campaign, you can determine whether your narrative has persuaded customers to upgrade to more costly options or add more items to their basket. As a result, the average order value will rise.

Suggestion: Consider using narrative elements that highlight the benefits and value of pricier products or offering bundled deals that encourage customers to spend more money to raise the average order value (AOV).

3. **Value of a Customer over Time (CLTV):** This metric helps ascertain the long-term value of each client. It takes into account the revenue a customer generates while interacting with your brand. By keeping an eye on the CLTV, you can determine how your brand storytelling influences customer loyalty and repeat business.

For example, let's say you decide to use a brand storytelling strategy that stresses building a connection with your target audience on an emotional level. Through the use of CLTV monitoring, which results in recurring business and more in-depth interactions with your establishment, you may determine whether your storytelling efforts have been successful in building customer loyalty.

Suggestion: To increase CLTV, consider running recurrent storytelling campaigns that strengthen relationships with customers and encourage repeat business. Customer loyalty can be fostered and CLTV rose with the use of loyalty programs, exclusive content, and personalized email marketing.

Case Study: The Nike "Dream Crazy" ad is among the best illustrations of how narrative can boost conversions. For the ad, Colin Kaepernick narrated a beautiful film that emphasized the importance of pursuing one's passions and having lofty goals. Despite the controversy surrounding the advertisement, Nike reported a noticeable increase in sales; online sales increased by 31% as soon as the campaign was launched. This case study illustrates how measurable results, like increased sales and conversion rates, may be obtained through excellent storytelling.

By keeping an eye on conversion numbers, you may gain crucial insights into the effectiveness of your brand storytelling campaigns. These metrics provide a practical way to assess the success of your storytelling endeavors and assist you in making well-informed decisions to enhance the storytelling strategy for your brand. These analytics include tracking client lifetime value, average order values, and conversion rates.

5. **Metric-Based Assessment of Loyalty and Brand Advocacy**

The success or failure of your brand storytelling endeavors will depend on factors such as brand advocacy and loyalty. Consumers need to do more than just be aware of your brand; they need to interact with it, promote it, and take action. Metrics show how well your brand storytelling strategies are functioning, which makes them crucial for assessing brand advocacy and loyalty. Here are some important metrics to consider:

1. **Net Promoter Score (NPS)**: This widely used metric evaluates customer loyalty and advocacy. Based on how they respond to a simple question, "On a scale of 0-10, how likely are you to recommend our brand to others?" customers are divided into three groups. Detractors (0–6), Passives (7-8), and Promoters (9–10). By deducting the percentage of Detractors from the percentage of Promoters, you may calculate the overall advocacy and loyalty level within your client base.

For example, a clothing manufacturer uses brand loyalty to calculate NPS. They find that 10% of their customers are Detractors, 30% are Passives, and 60% are Promoters. This implies a high level of brand advocacy and commitment among their clientele.

Advice: To improve your net promoter score (NPS), focus on addressing the concerns raised by detractors and winning over those who are opposed to you. Talk with customers about their experiences and follow up on their suggestions.

2. Customer Lifetime Value (CLV) is a statistic that measures the total value a customer adds to your company throughout their relationship with you. It takes into account factors like the average purchase amount, frequency of purchases, and customer

retention rate. By examining CLV, you can find loyal customers who significantly contribute to the success of your business.

An example of this would be an online subscription firm that calculates the CLV of its subscribers and discovers that those who have been with them for more than a year have a significantly higher CLV than those who have recently joined. This highlights how important it is to build long-lasting relationships with customers to increase brand loyalty and advocacy.

Offer personalized experiences, loyalty plans, and excellent customer service to increase customer satisfaction and CLV.

3. **Social Media Engagement**: Advocacy and brand loyalty can be accurately predicted by the volume of engagement on social media platforms. Metrics such as likes, shares, comments, and mentions provide you with insights into your customers' interaction with your brand's content and their propensity to share it with others.

Case Study: Product recommendations and makeup tutorials are actively shared by consumers, according to social media engagement metrics monitored by a beauty company. By finding them, the company may collaborate with these brand advocates to expand their reach and influence.

Encourage the sharing of user-generated material and create interesting content that your target audience will want to share. Engage with customers on social media and respond to their queries and comments promptly to foster a sense of community.

Finally, you may use analytics to assess brand advocacy and loyalty to determine how well your brand storytelling strategies are working. Using metrics like NPS, CLV, and social media involvement, you can identify advocates, enhance brand loyalty, and foster organic development. These metrics offer useful information.

6. Evaluating Social Media KPIs to Create a Powerful Brand Story

1. **Rate of Engagement**: The engagement rate is one of the most important metrics to consider when evaluating the success of your brand storytelling efforts on social media. This metric evaluates the level of interaction and engagement your audience has with your content. Included are likes, comments, shares, and all other forms of interaction with your postings. A high rate of engagement indicates that your target audience is engaged and captivated by the story of your brand. If a particular post that outlines your brand's beliefs and mission receives a considerably higher engagement rate than other posts, for example, it means that your storytelling efforts are effectively engaging your target audience.

2. **Impressions and Reach**: When evaluating the overall visibility and exposure of your brand's storytelling endeavors, these two KPIs are essential. Reach is the total number of unique people who have

visited your content, while impressions are the total number of times it has been presented. By monitoring these metrics, you may ascertain the number of individuals your brand is interacting with and the extent to which its message is disseminated. When a new brand narrative campaign is launched, for instance, and reach and impressions suddenly rise, it indicates that more people are viewing and sharing your content, which increases brand awareness.

3. **Conversion Rate**: Producing conversions is ultimately what makes your brand storytelling efforts effective, even though reach and engagement are important as well. The conversion rate is the proportion of visitors who, after engaging with your brand's story, finish a desired action (such as completing a purchase, signing up for a newsletter, or downloading an e-book). By keeping an eye on this signal, you can determine whether your storytelling is effectively inspiring your audience to take action. For example, when you release a brand storytelling film and see a significant increase in conversions, your storytelling approach is working and compelling.

Sentiment analysis: Social media platforms provide valuable insights into how your audience views the narrative efforts that your business has undertaken. Sentiment analysis is the act of monitoring and assessing the viewpoints presented in user-generated content, like comments and reviews. This indication helps you assess whether the narrative surrounding your brand is well received and, if not, what needs to be changed. When reviews and comments regarding a particular brand storytelling campaign, for instance, have a high percentage of positive sentiment, it indicates that your audience connects with your story and that your brand is perceived more favorably.

Suggestions for Evaluating Social Media KPIs for Effective Brand Narration:

Establish clear goals: Before evaluating social media analytics, create specific goals for your campaigns that tell tales about your companies. This will make it possible for you to accurately evaluate success and align your metrics with your objectives.

- **Use reliable analytics tools**: Reliable analytics tools are essential for effectively tracking, analyzing, and assessing social media data. Platforms like Sprout Social, Hoot suite, and Google Analytics offer deep insights into sentiment analysis, engagement, reach, and conversions.

- **Benchmark and compare**: Evaluate your social media KPIs regularly by comparing them to previous attempts and industry standards. This helps you to identify areas that require improvement and make fact-based decisions to enhance your brand storytelling efforts.

A Case Study of Nike's "Dream Crazy" Campaign

The "Dream Crazy" campaign by Colin Kaepernick for Nike is a fantastic example of how to use social media to effectively communicate a brand's story. The program aimed to empower individuals to pursue their dreams despite social limitations. Nike evaluated several social media metrics to determine the success of the campaign:

- **Engagement Rate**: Nike's "Dream Crazy" campaign dramatically increased the engagement rate across all of their social media channels. The campaign's potent message and thought-provoking material sparked thousands of likes, comments, and shares, sparking meaningful conversations.

- **Reach and Impressions**: The campaign reached millions of users globally, significantly raising its profile. Nike collaborated with influencers and strategically used hashtags to expand the brand story material's reach and impression count.

- **Conversion Rate**: Nike's online traffic and sales both experienced notable increases during the campaign. Users were prompted to purchase Nike goods and engage with the brand more via a compelling call to action and compelling storytelling.

Using Metrics for Brand Storytelling to Drive Long-Term Success:

Despite some controversy around the advertisement, sentiment

In today's competitive business climate, brands seeking to build a stronger relationship with their target audience have found that brand storytelling is a critical tactic. However, telling compelling stories is not enough on its own. If you want to be able to evaluate the success of your brand storytelling efforts, you must use the right metrics. By keeping an eye on critical variables, businesses can make data-driven decisions that support long-term performance and provide valuable insights into the effectiveness of their storytelling efforts.

1. **One of the most important metrics to consider when evaluating the performance of your brand narrative is conversion rates**. One way to measure the effectiveness of your storytelling is to look at the number of people who interact with the story of your brand and then complete the intended action, such as making a purchase, downloading an e-book, or subscribing to your newsletter. For example, when you initiate a fresh brand narrative campaign and witness a rise in conversion rates, it indicates that your audience identifies with your narrative and is motivated to take action.

2. **Engagement Metrics**: These metrics are yet another crucial category to consider. These metrics let you assess the degree to which your target audience is being captivated and engaged by your brand narrative. Engagement indicators include things like how long visitors spend on your website, bounce rates, shares,

likes, and comments on social media. For example, if the average time visitors spend on your brand narrative blog articles is high, it means that your storytelling is compelling enough to hold their interest.

3. **Brand Awareness**: Brand awareness is a crucial metric for gauging the success of your brand storytelling campaigns. By keeping an eye on metrics like website traffic, social media followers, and search engine results, you can gauge the level of awareness your business has generated through storytelling. For example, if you see a significant increase in organic search traffic and social media followers after releasing a brand story film, your storytelling has been successful in increasing brand visibility and awareness.

4. **Customer feedback**: This is an invaluable resource for determining how well your brand's story is working. Whether it comes from surveys, reviews, or comments on social media, collecting and analyzing customer feedback can help you understand more about how your story resonates with your target audience. If you receive good feedback and testimonials from your customers that demonstrate how your brand story has impacted their viewpoint and purchase decisions, for instance, your brand narrative is having a lasting impact on them.

5. **Case Study**: Let's investigate the efficacy of applying brand storytelling analytics using a clothes company that has launched a new brand narrative campaign. Through close examination of their

conversion rates, engagement data, and brand recognition, the most effective elements of their storytelling strategy were identified. By conducting A/B testing of different storylines and analyzing the resulting analytics, they discovered that the most compelling and successful conversion rates originated from personal stories that their customers posted on social media. Armed with this insight, the business consistently employed customer stories in their advertisements, enabling them to optimize their narrative approach and secure sustained prosperity.

In conclusion, assessing the success of your brand storytelling initiatives requires a systematic and data-driven approach. Using the surveillance of diverse measures such as consumer feedback, brand awareness, engagement metrics, conversion rates, and brand awareness, entities can acquire substantial insights into the effectiveness of their narrative strategies. Armed with this knowledge, companies can make informed decisions to optimize their brand story and promote long-term success.

Chapter 8:

Why Brand Storytelling Is Essential for the Future of Marketing

There are almost 42 million SMEs in India. A considerable number of small business owners are unaware of the concept of brand storytelling, let alone how to make use of it.

What is brand storytelling exactly, and how can it help your business?

The Basics of Brand Storytelling

Before you begin writing your novel, you must clearly define your goal. Your goal is to establish a relationship with both current and potential clients. You can humanize your brand by providing customers with a reason to do business with you in the first place and to continue doing so.

Consumers care about product quality, but to win them over to your brand, you also need to emotionally connect with them.

Brand storytelling, to put it briefly, is a cohesive narrative that links the specifics and emotions a brand arouses. Through all of their channels of communication, businesses should start talking about the larger picture of their brand, such as why it exists, in addition to providing customers with incentives to buy a good or service. Why does that matter?

Putting Your Story Together

As a brand, you may talk about a wide range of subjects. It's easy to feel overwhelmed by the sheer number of stories you have at your disposal.

You start to think about which story will work the best and produce the best results.

Put Your Brand's Principles First

Consumers like to deal with and support those who share their ideals in life. It could be disconcerting to put your ideals on display for everyone to see. You might worry that people would think poorly of you and decide to do business with someone else.

You might lose some people by standing up for your principles, but the people you gain will far exceed the people you lose.

If you are unsure of how to express your convictions, get together with your business companions and determine which values are true to your company. After you become aware of anything, think about how it seems.

What acts does your company implement in light of these principles? People will realize that you are living it rather than just talking about it when you tell them about it.

Go Back in Time

Talking about how and why you started your company and how it evolved to its present stage can be inspiring. When you embrace your origins, the right individuals will be drawn to your story.

Know Who Your Audience Is

If you want to tell your narrative effectively, you should think about your audience. For a brand to be successful, it needs to grow into much more than just a line of products or services.

When speaking with millennial, you will approach the topic differently than when speaking with married, family-oriented audience members.

Make sure the story appeals to the individual you are conversing with if you want the greatest result. Once your audience feels comfortable and confident in you, your chances of closing deals will soar, and you will have made lasting impressions at the very least.

Profits and the Human Aspect

Brand tales can have a significant impact. They can help you differentiate yourself from the competition and boost revenue in addition to putting you in front of the clients you want to attract.

Consumers need proof that companies are changing the world, contributing to charitable causes, and achieving goals beyond just generating money. Ironically, to motivate them to make larger purchases, buyers want to know that a company has values beyond profitability. It is probably no coincidence that the 10 wealthiest and fastest-growing companies in the world are also the most compassionate, as ranked by the Global Empathy Index.

So what actions can one do to make their brand more relatable? Storytelling is the answer, once more.

Remember to incorporate the bigger story into your marketing strategies: Why are you more approachable? How do you impact and transform other people's lives? What positive contributions do you make to society?

Don't dance around customer issues

Customers are buying your products to solve problems. You can't act as though there isn't a problem. It is not necessary to create a scenario where everything goes smoothly.

It's not always the case that what customers find appealing today will match the challenges you set out to answer with your product. Instead of assuming that customers still receive the same advantages from your products or services, look through social media, customer testimonials, and polls.

Treating these pain locations shouldn't always be done in the same way. Think about several ways to address the things that are bothering you the most.

Find out what the future holds for branding and marketing.

This article examines the marketing and branding trends for 2024 that you shouldn't ignore if you want to expand your business and establish a memorable brand.

Whether you are a seasoned pro or just starting, you need to include the newest branding and marketing trends in your plan to stay relevant and competitive in today's industry.

An educated brand marketing strategy is the cornerstone of a powerful brand and, consequently, of a prosperous company.

Plans and Patterns

As the future of marketing draws nearer, the art of brand storytelling is evolving into a science. Rather than focusing just on a product or service, today's consumers want a deeper connection with businesses. In a world where consumers' attention spans are increasingly shorter, creating an authentic and captivating brand story is crucial to grabbing and retaining their interest.

Multiple cutting-edge methods and trends are influencing how brand storytelling will develop in the future. For example, customization is now necessary rather than discretionary. Businesses can utilize customer data to craft customized stories that establish a deeper connection with individual clients.

Interesting Content

Interactive content is drastically altering the landscape of digital marketing by cutting through the constant cacophony of advertising to create deeper, more meaningful connections with viewers.

Companies may create captivating experiences to entice new consumers and keep hold of existing ones. Gamified stories that allow users to actively engage in the storytelling process and quiz that provide informative data about preferences and habits are two examples of these kinds of experiences.

User-Generated Content (UGC): In recent times, UGC has gained significant traction as a powerful medium for fostering brand-audience relationships.

Users now can create and share content through social media, including textual blogs, videos, and photos. By supporting and encouraging user-generated content (UGC), brands can take advantage of the creativity and enthusiasm of their customers and create a feeling of community around their products.

Short-Form Video: Thanks to social media platforms like Instagram and TikTok, short-form videos have become more and more popular as a form of content.

One of the main benefits of short-form video is its ability to reach a larger audience. Because consumers have shorter attention spans, they are more likely to interact with brand content that is concise and visually appealing.

Brands that use short-form videos to tell an engaging story can strengthen their emotional connection with viewers and foster enduring loyalty.

By applying these new trends and tactics, you can craft a true and captivating brand story that will captivate your audience and make you stand out in the years to come.

Are you having problems carrying out your strategy or plan? Whether you are an established business or a startup, Tally can help you engage your audience and convey your story in a year and beyond.

REVIEW